How to Climb Your Family Tree

How to Climb Your Family Tree

Without Going Out on a Limb

A Guide To Family History

Elizabeth Queener

Eggman Publishing, Inc., 2909 Poston Avenue, Suite 203,
Nashville, TN 37203.

Edited by Richard Courtney.

Printed in the United States of America.
First Trade Printing: November, 1994

Cover Design by The Pure Idea Workshop, Nashville, Tennessee

Design and Typography by Mike Walker

ISBN: 0-9635026-9-7

INTRODUCTION

The purpose of this guide is to aid the beginning researcher in discovering a personal, fascinating heritage. As you delve into your background, you will develop a deeply-felt sense of appreciation for your ancestry. Once-dull pages of history will come alive as you become acquainted with your ancestors and their lives. *How To Climb Your Family Tree Without Going Out On A Limb* will save you time, frustration, and effort as you walk back through history. A true and accurate accounting of your past will direct your future and give pride and purpose to your life. With thanks to

Meade Frierson,
    Birmingham, Alabama
Paul LeMasters,
    Kingston, Tennessee
My Gene Pool

Contents

CHAPTER ONE

Getting Started and Using the Chart

In compiling a family history, organization is vital. The chart on the back cover provides a concise, uncomplicated way to record the information you unearth as you perform your research. This chart is easy to use for registering the data you gather for piecing together your heritage. Make multiple copies of this chart and enlarge or modify it as needed. When you complete the four generations on your first chart, begin a new chart for each of the last eight people on your original chart. In other words, each of your great-grandparents will begin a new chart. After you have completed nine charts, you will have documented seven generations and developed an intimacy with the last two hundred years as you discovered the lives of your ancestors, where they lived and the drama of their lives.

To begin your quest, first collect all information you possibly can about your family from family members, friends and acquaintances; especially the older ones. Use your best interviewing techniques to stimulate their memory. It is most important you record all information by taking notes or by tape. Make copies of any information they may be able to provide from Bibles, diaries or other family mementoes. This information will be the foundation of your research and should take you through the first three generations.

Should you be adopted and know the circumstances of your birth and the names of your biological parents you can request a copy of their birth certificates from The Bureau of Vital Statistics in the capital of the state where they were born. The more information you have, the better as to county or parish of their birth and year of birth. When you receive their birth certificates, you will, more than likely, receive a bonus - the names of their parents.

The fourth generation is, for most persons, the first place to stumble. The following are important tools for family research.

Important Tools for Researching Your Family Tree

BIRTH CERTIFICATES

Birth certificates are available from every state. Dates of Availability vary with each state. A call or note to The Bureau of Vital Statistics at the state capital will get you the necessary information and forms to complete.

CENSUS RECORDS

Census records hold some of the most valuable tools for researching your family tree.

The earliest United States Census was taken in 1790. States compiled were the original Thirteen Colonies, which comprised an area of seventeen present states. These states are Connecticut, Maine, Maryland,

New York, Massachusetts, New Hampshire, New Jersey, Pennsylvania, Virginia, North Carolina, Rhode Island, South Carolina, Delaware, Georgia, Kentucky, Tennessee, and Vermont. Unfortunately, some of these records have been destroyed - some by the British during the War of 1812 and some through carelessness at the local level. The states affected are Delaware, Georgia, Kentucky, New Jersey, Tennessee, and Virginia.

The original Thirteen Colony States have Colonial census records which are quite informative. Some states, such as Virginia, conducted a census before Congress authorized one nationwide. In Virginia, a census was conducted in 1782, 1783, 1784, and 1785. Also, the colonies kept tax-lists, wills, real-estate transfers and other legal documents.

Until 1850, Census records gave only the name of the head of the family, the number of family members by age group and sex, and the number of slaves owned by the family head. The 1850 Census, however, expanded on this information and listed not only the names of each person in the household, but also their occupation, the value of their real estate and personal property, their place of birth, their parents' place of birth, and their literacy. In 1850, all free persons of color were listed by name with accompanying information.

Census records are available only through 1920 as a privacy law seals the records for seventy-two years. There are no census records for 1890 as the records were consumed by a fire in the Department of Commerce in Washington.

You will be glad to know that many census records are alphabetized and are easy to use. You can find all census records at the National Archives in Washington or at any of their field branches. Field branches of the National Archives are located in Atlanta, Boston, New York, Philadelphia, Chicago, Kansas City, Fort Worth, Denver, Los Angeles, San Francisco, and Seattle. An annex to the National Archives will be located in Maryland and is scheduled to open in 1996. The new annex in suburban Washington will provide state of the art research facilities. Copies of census can also be found at the various state archives and to a lesser degree and more localized at various libraries throughout the country.

Strategy: You know your grandfather, Jean Lafitte Chasebaum was born in St. Tammany Parish, Louisiana, sometime between 1901 and 1904. At the library, find the Louisiana Census for 1910 and look for the returns for St. Tammany Parish. Hopefully, they will be alphabetized and you will easily check each Chasebaum family until you find the one that records a seven year old son named Jean Lafitte. Not only will you find little Jean Lafitte, you will find his parents and siblings and a bunch of information about them.

NEWSPAPERS

If you have an important date for someone, i.e., their birth, marriage, death or other event, newspapers can provide you with a wealth of information. A marriage announcement or obituary will give family, spouses, and down right gossip in sometimes flowery prose. In the old days, society editors waxed romantically about beautiful brides and gorgeous dresses. Pedigrees were revealed as well as occupations. What you want to do is check the local paper on the date of the event and a few days hence. Careful reading can give you insight into the lives of the persons you are researching. Most local libraries have newspapers on file dating back in the 1800's and you can find more extensive collections at state archives on microfilm. Newspaper morgues generally have back copies on file for many years.

CHURCH AND CEMETERY RECORDS

More often than not, churches and synagogues keep records of marriages, births, baptisms, and burials. A call or visit to a church once attended by an ancestor can reveal a treasure trove of information. It can also prove to be a stirring experience to be in the place where your ancestors worshiped, or to stand at their graves.

Tombstones record information chiseled in the stone that might otherwise have been lost.

MILITARY RECORDS

Millions of Americans have served their country in the military from the time of the Revolution. If you have names and dates, service records can be researched at the National Archives, one of their branches, or the state or locality in which the person lived. The National Archives will send a record of military service. This address is in the last chapter of this book.

FAMILY HISTORY LIBRARY
THE CHURCH OF JESUS CHRIST
OF LATTER DAY SAINTS

The Family History Library was founded by the Latter Day Saints in 1894 in Salt Lake City, Utah. It has grown to astonishing proportions, currently housing thousands of family histories in book form and a computer network of over ten million names. This is an amazing resource which can be utilized by calling your local Church of Jesus Christ of Latter Day Saints as to location, hours of service, and availability of records, as they have genealogical libraries in many cities. Their records also include foreign countries.

STATE AND LOCAL RECORDS

Each state has a State Archive and Library which will provide limited research by mail. It is best to call before writing to ascertain the extent of their service. State, county, and town records are fascinating in the information they store. In the thirteen colony states, information can be found about your ancestors in colonial times.

When wills are read, personalities suddenly come alive. You can discover where they lived, if they were involved in litigation, and feel involved in a novel as their lives unfold. Most states, counties, and towns have local history and genealogical societies which publish periodicals, collect records, and are helpful to persons seeking information. Some of these organizations, such as the Daughters of the American Revolution,

The Colonial Dames, and The New England Historic Genealogical Society have extensive records.

IMMIGRATION AND NATURALIZATION RECORDS

The National Archives has records relating to arrivals from 1798. However, most records concern arrivals dating from the year 1815. There was no law requiring arrival information about persons coming into the country from Canada or Mexico during the 19th Century. Most ship lists are from the period of 1815-1915 with arrival into Atlantic and Gulf Ports. There are books dealing with records dating from the 17th Century and a list will be given in the last chapter. It is always thrilling to find an ancestor on a passenger list, and you should research this area diligently. Every library will have indexed books with passenger arrivals, The thirteen original states likewise have information on arrivals at their ports.

For naturalization during colonial times, you should consult the records of the original colony state. After 1790, aliens were required to apply and receive citizenships in a court of law. This law has varied from time to time as to procedure. These can be found in part locally, in part at the National Archives, or in the records of the respective district courts. They are difficult to find and, unless you know exactly when and where your ancestor arrived and lived, the search may be lengthy. There are a number of books relating to specific periods and places which you can find at your state library.

COMPUTER PROGRAMS

There are many family history software programs on the market which are becoming more popular as they are improved. If you have the capacity, there is also CD ROM research available. An especially interesting CD ROM has been developed by Automated Archives, Inc. They offer data from as far back as Colonial tax lists up to recent social security lists. Catalogues are available for this service which can produce results quickly. The Latter Day Saints

Church computer program, Personal Ancestral File, is an amazing compilation of hundreds of thousands of family histories. Amazingly, the Church of Jesus Christ of Latter Day Saints main frame in Salt Lake City can, through Internet and Compuserve for instance, search and assemble five thousand references of a surname in a matter of seconds and send them back through telephone lines to your hard disk. In that way, you can browse through them.

To receive information on this program, call: 1-801-240-2584, the Family History Department of The Church of Jesus Christ of Latter Day Saints.

Development of this field will make research in the future much easier.

CHAPTER TWO

Who Were All Those People?

My Grandparents' Grandparents

The best advice for anyone attempting to climb their family tree is: *Don't panic!* You *can* find your ancestors. Almost everyone has been a part of some kind of record.

After exhausting friends and relatives' memories and records, I again urge you to visit an ancestral cemetery and carefully read tombstones of family members. Valuable information is often chiseled onto crypts and stones. Additionally, cemeteries are places of romance and mystery where one is able to escape the clamor of modern life. It is quite possible to visit the grave of an ancestor who fought to establish the United States, then turn to face the resting place of his grandson who fought to divide it.

Should the cemetery you seek not be just around the corner, you can write or call the caretaker or administrator of the particular cemetery in which you are interested and ask them to send you a copy of the script on your ancestor's stone. With your request, provide the caretaker with the name and date of death. A funeral director can also perform this service.

At this point in your research, I must advise you to be flexible about the spelling of surnames. You may be looking for your great-grandfather John Cain and run across families named Kane, Cane, and Caine. Examine the records for all possible spellings, as your Cain may indeed have been spelled differently a few generations ago.

One important trick to remember is the "middle and given name speculation theory." Employing this theory may provide clues to many of the dilemmas you may encounter in your search for your ancestors. Carefully examine the middle names of your predecessors. Could Webster Gordon Hampton be named for a Grandfather Webster? Or, could it be a Grandmother Gordon or even a Great Grandfather Webster or Great Grandmother Gordon?

Whereas for generations family research was a Caucasian preserve, primarily for proof of heritage of admission to a patriotic society or to impress the in-laws, Alex Haley changed that. If you are African American, remember there were thousands of free persons of color in the United States prior to the War Between the States and they are recorded in legal documents, tax lists, etc. Civil War records of black soldiers fighting on both sides are particularly fascinating and easily available. In addition, there is an African American Genealogical Association. The address is listed at the back of this publication with other useful addresses. Many wills of slave owners listed the names of their slaves who generally took their owners' names which have been handed down to the present.

Visiting the Library
How does it stack up?

WHERE TO GO

Your best library this side of Washington, D.C., where the National Archives, The Library of Congress, and the Daughters of the American Revolution Libraries are located, is the closest library with a genealogical or local history section. Each state has a state library and archives. Eventually, that is where you need to be.

Before your visit to the library of your choice, pack your tools in a brief case or tote bag if you are allowed to enter with more than a pencil and tablet. You will need your completed charts, some unused charts, and all loose information on your family, including notes containing hints from Great Aunt Hortense such as "I think the Browns came from North Carolina after the Revolutionary War."

By now you should have organized family folders on the front of which you have drawn a family tree relative to that branch. Tucked away you will have pencils with good erasers, notebooks, dimes and quarters for copy machines, and, if you become a zealot, a lap-top computer and a cellular telephone for hushed calls to Great Aunt Hortense inquiring if she ever heard anyone mention a Mortimer Caine, a.k.a. Mattie Sue Kane, a cross-dressing bank robber who terrorized the Ohio Valley in the 1840s.

WHAT TO EXPECT

Upon entering the library to begin your search, you should have your information and work tools neatly assembled. Be forewarned! You may well be stopped by a black belt matron who will require you to sign an entrance card, secure a search card, and sign an oath you will not remove historical records or memorabilia from the building stashed under your toupee or stuffed in your blouse. After this warm welcome, you will be allowed to enter.

Your next move is to stand at the information desk and look intelligent. Eventually, someone will look up from their work or emerge from the stacks. The ice will be broken either by the staff person inquiring why you are standing there or by you uttering what you hope is a lucid remark. At this time, you should slowly and clearly state your purpose. For instance, "Hello, I'm doing family research. Let me show you where I've gotten and you can tell me how to proceed." Flash your chart and your smile.

A helpful librarian might offer "Oh, you've traced back to your great grandparents on both sides. I suggest that after you've looked in our family history section to see if there is any published work on any of these families, then look in our county history section. Our census records are on the desk in the middle of the hall and our indexes are in the corridor to the right of the entrance to the building. The index includes all of our books ranging from what is available in the public areas to what is available in the stacks. We have books and microfilm of most census schedules, military records for the American Revolution. War of 1812, The Mexican War, The Civil War, The Indian Wars and the Spanish American War, state histories, city histories, tax lists and colonial records including the French and Indian Wars. If I can get you anything, it will be my pleasure," or something to that effect.

With a smile and a sense of anticipation, you make your way towards a reading table. Choose an empty one, if possible, as you will want to spread your notes around you for you will soon be surrounded by a dozen or more books. Sit down and settle in. The best advice I can give you now as you proceed to dive into serious research is: SEE IF SOMEONE ELSE HAS ALREADY DONE IT!

Your first act is to go, as the librarian advised, to the family history section and see if a distant cousin in Des Moines has spent a lifetime and a fortune gathering all known facts and a bit of fiction on a branch of your family. In this case, you look for books on the families of Cain, Blaine, Paine, and

Saine. You find books on Kane, Payne, Paine, Cane, and Blaine.

You quickly eliminate by reason of geography and dates all books but, *The Life and Times of Charity and Moses Paine of the Bloody Creek Community of Hickman County, Tennessee* by Blaine Paine, Judge, General Sessions Court, Hickman County, Tennessee, 1936. Aquiver with excitement and with trembling hands, you open the musty-smelling book. Moments later, recovering from the hair-raising sight of a photograph of Charity and Moses in work clothes leaning on hoes in front of a moonshine still, circa 1902, you proceed to the text.

God bless Judge Blaine Paine. Not only has he provided you with Charity and Moses you have found your Grandfather listed as the grandson of Mr. and Mrs. Paine with the word "*vanished*" beside his name. "Vanished no more," you think.

CHAPTER THREE

Johnny Reb and Union Jack

You may have four or more ancestors who could have had service in either the Confederate or Union army. In many cases, especially in the border states of Tennessee, North Carolina, Kentucky and Arkansas, you may have ancestors fighting against one another.

Most Union soldiers served in the volunteer force of the United States while a minority served in the regular army. Should you know the name, branch of service, state from which he enlisted, or other information regarding your ancestor, you can find his service record and pension record at the National Archives. Looking for a Union soldier can be facilitated by looking in The Official Register of the Volunteer Force of the United States for the Years 1861-65.

Separate indexes are available for each state with the exception of South Carolina, which furnished no soldiers to the U.S. Army. Once again, state and local records should be located. From these sources you receive valuable information as to details of service, wounds, imprisonment, and discharge. Local records provide colorful personal information. Each state has information regarding their Union Jacks and Johnny Rebs.

When Richmond was abandoned, all Confederate military records were taken to Charlotte, North Carolina. Subsequently, they were taken by the United States Army to Washington where they were put under the jurisdiction of the War Department. These records have been copied as compiled service records of Confederate soldiers who served in organizations raised directly by the Confederate Government. The information includes battle duty, age, employment, rank, and a physical description. In addition, each Southern state provides pensions for their native sons and pension applications can be found in their state archives. Again, you would need to know basic facts such as name, state, and branch of service. It is generally easier to find your Johnny Reb among the records of local Southern Archives.

The War Between the States gave birth to the publication of memoirs, diaries, and journals. Also, sites of battles have information at hand locally.

CHAPTER FOUR

Those Blank Spots in the Middle

Eventually you will reach the point where you have exhausted all resources in locating a particular ancestor. You may even think you know their name but you cannot get the proof. Most clues to their identity have come up empty of fact.

At this point you may consider hiring a professional genealogist to assist you. A sensible way to chose a genealogist is to contact the state library and archives of the resident state and have a list of genealogists sent to you. When you receive it, note if there is anyone offering their services in the town or county where the missing portion of your family lived. Call or write this person and ask for their fee schedule in writing. If the cost for their services seems reasonable, hire them, but put a cap on charges. Provide the searcher with all the information you have compiled pertinent to your mystery ancestors presented in a neat, straightforward way. This will prevent duplication of service and make your funds go further. Ask for a review when one-third of your proposed funds are depleted and, at that time, you can determine whether or not to continue.

Many genealogists are now certified, which means they have received advanced training at approved facilities. One such facility is the Family History Library of the Church of Jesus Christ of Latter Day Saints, the mecca for all devotees of family history. There are, however, scores of genealogists who are not certified but have been doing research for years who are very competent and do good work.

Research can also be undertaken to varying degrees by the staff at state archives as well as the National Archives.

CHAPTER FIVE

Save Your Life With Genealogical Research: Creating A Genetic Health Profile

With daily announcements of advances in genetic links to physical problems and the advancement of tests to determine weaknesses and treatments in risk patients, an accurate knowledge of our ancestors' health can prolong and enhance our life. Every one should have an ancestral Earth profile. In the *New York Times*, (September 20, 1994), Dr. Mark Skolnick, whose team at the University of Utah discovered the gene that causes inherited breast cancer, attributed his success to "hard work, missteps by competitors and **the vast genealogical archives of the Mormon Church in Salt Lake City.**"

Beginning in 1850, the United States Government compiled mortality schedules which give the following information for each American citizen who died during the first half of 1850:

Age and place of birth

Color — divided into white, black, mulatto

Marital status

Cause, date of death, and length of illness

Occupation.

This census was repeated for 1860 and in 1870, was expanded to include Chinese or Indian and information as to whether or not parents were foreign born. In 1880, the mortality schedule was further expanded to show length of residence in the United States, parents' birthplace, location disease was contracted, and name of physician.

Family Bibles, local death certificates of more recent ancestors, obituaries in newspapers and undertakers' records are also sources for this information. If a military pension was awarded a surviving spouse, the form will give death information to some degree.

Using the above techniques, you can easily chart weaknesses and strengths in a family line. In this instance, an interest in family history can become a life saver.

How to Climb Your Family Tree

CHAPTER SIX

Reorganizing and Sharpening Goals

On your next trip to the library, you have to make some hardline decisions. On your original trek, you were seeking information on four families in Hickman County, Tennessee. Coupling Lady Luck with your intelligence, you have added seven new lines to the original three. Do you go back to the original three, or do you take off on a heady tangent with your newly-discovered early American families?

As you delve more deeply into your genealogy, it is easy to get sidetracked or overwhelmed by all of the information readily available to you. However, the best strategy is to complete your initial goal before taking on even greater obstacles. STAY FOCUSED.

My advice, therefore, is to go back to

the original three and get their lines completely in order. Remember, every generation doubles with ancestors, and, at this point, you must take first things first. All of that other information is not going anywhere. It will still be available when you get around to it. So, take it one generation at a time.

Goals ignite the light at the end of the tunnel and provide the possibilities of closure. A few suggestions are as follows:

(1) Find all Civil War Ancestors with military service

(2) Find all War of 1812 ancestors with military service

(3) Find all Revolutionary War Ancestors with military service

(4) Find French and Indian Wars ancestors with military records

(5) Find those who served in the colonial militia

(6) Complete seven generations

(7) Complete all lines to original settlers to United States

CHAPTER SEVEN

Summing it Up—
Who Am I?

As you conduct your research and fill in the blank spots on your charts, your spirits soar for you will have reached out and touched the past. As an American, you have discovered the various cultures that have come together to make you unique. A part of you can be a native American girl married to a French trapper or a Spanish Conquistador. You may ponder the fate of the Dutch sea captain lost in a storm leaving behind a widow and a young daughter destined to marry a wealthy planter. Perhaps, an ancestor was seized in Africa and brought to bondage in America surviving by courage and intelligence. You question the relationship of two ancestors, enemies during the War Between the States living three miles apart in peace after the conflict, and you feel pride for the widowed pioneer woman who raised six children on the frontier. Whether they were dirt poor or land proud, Okies or Wall Street tycoons, wild Celts, dancing Cajuns, or shackled slaves intoning their spirituals, they make you what you are today.

You may never fill in all the blanks for there are those lost to history. But, like the unknown soldier at Arlington, they are remembered by their mystery.

Enjoy your heritage and appreciate the past.

HELPFUL ADDRESSES AND BOOKS

BOOKS:

Original Lists of Persons of Quality, Great Britain to America 1600-1700, Baltimore, Genealogical Publishing Co., 1974

Jewish Immigration from 1881-1910, Joseph, Samuel. New York, Arno Press, 1967.

Passengers and Immigration (lists Index, 500,000 passengers to US and Canada in the 17th, 18th, 19th Century. Three volumes; Annual supplements. Detroit, Gale Research Co, 1981)

Genealogical Research in the National Archives, National Archives Trust Fund Board, Washington, D.C.; Secure from Archives: 7th and Penn Street, Washington, DC 20408

Searching for Your Ancestors; Doane & Gilbert, University of Minnesota, Minneapolis, 1980.

Genealogical Research, Methods, and Sources; American Society of Genealogists, Volume 2; Revised Editions, Edited by Stryker-Rodda, Washington, DC.

The Researcher's Guide to American Genealogy; Greenwood Genealogical Publishing Company, 1983.

How To Trace Your Family Tree: A Basic Guide To Genealogy. Linder, Everest House, New York.

ADDRESSES:

Any state Archives and library, Capitol of State.

Family History Library of the Church of Jesus Christ of Latter Day Saints,
35 Northwest Temple Street
Salt Lake City, Utah 84150
Telephone: 801/240-2331

Library of Congress
Family History Department Annex
1st-2nd Street SE
Washington, DC 20540

Afro-American Historical and Genealogist Society
P.O. Box 73086
Washington, DC 20056

National Archives and Records
General Reference Branch
7th & Penn Avenue NW
Washington, DC 20408
**For military records prior to 1917 ask for
Form: NATF 80

Daughters of the American Revolution
1776 D. Street NW
Washington, DC 20006-5392

Brother's Keeper
6907 Chilsdale Rd.
Rockford, MI 49341
616-866-9422

Everyone's Family Tree
The Dollarhide Systems, Inc.
203 West Holly St. M-4
Bellingham, WA 98225
206-671-3808

Family Origins
Parson's Technology
P.O. Box 100
Hiawatha, IA 52233-0100

Family Reunion
FAMware
1580 East Dawn Drive
Salt Lake City, UT 84121

Family Roots
Quinsept, Inc.
P.O. Box 216
Lexington, MA 02173
617-641-2930

Family Tree Maker
Banner Blue Software, Inc.
P.O. Box 7865
Fremont, CA 94537
415-794-6850

Personal Ancestral File
50 East North Temple
Salt Lake City, UT 84150
801-240-2548

Roots III & IV
COMMSOFT, Inc.
P.O. Box 310
Windsor, CA 95492
707-838-4300

The Family Edge Plus
Carl York
P.O. Box 3157
Knoxville, TN 37927
615-524-1702